The Houses We Build

by
LISL WEIL

Atheneum
1985
New York

Florist   Pizza

48819

J
28
W

To J E A N
and the joy of creating books

Library of Congress Cataloging in Publication Data

Weil, Lisl.
The houses we build.

SUMMARY: Surveys the variety of shelters made by
Western man, starting with the first move from caves to
tents and huts and showing the distinct style of
building developed by each successive civilization.
1. Dwellings—Juvenile literature. 2. Buildings—
Juvenile literature. [1. Dwellings. 2. Buildings]
I. Title.
TH4811.5.W35   1985   728′.09   84-21536
ISBN 0-689-31106-0

Published simultaneously in Canada by
McClelland & Stewart, Ltd.
Type set by Linoprint Composition, New York City
Printed and bound by Worzalla Publishing Company,
Stevens Point, Wisconsin
Designed by Mina Greenstein
First Edition

FOR each of us, everywhere, a house can be very special. Whether it is a sand castle or a real castle, a playhouse made of wooden blocks or a huge house made of cement blocks, a backyard tent made of an old blanket or a tent to live in, made of canvas or animal hides, a house is important to the person who lives there. It is a shelter, a place to think and rest and work and play. Fancy or plain, if it suits the people who use it, it is beautiful.

Just as we have real houses to live in, and maybe playhouses to play in, we also have dream houses that seem the very best kind of houses to us. Our dream houses express what we are as individuals. When I was young, I wanted to live in a huge tree, together with all my pets. And, of course, there would be room for my best friend to stay overnight.

Children, generally, cannot build their dream house. But in a way, adults do. The best houses express the dreams of the people who built them, sometimes individuals, and sometimes whole nations.

Not all houses, not all shelters, not all buildings that show people's thoughts and dreams, are places for living. Hospitals shelter people who are ill. Hotels shelter people who travel. Courthouse and city halls shelter people who have business with the law

and with government. Schools shelter people who need to learn. Churches shelter people who want to worship. Stores, offices and factories shelter businesses where people work.

Over the long years since people first began to build buildings, their ideas and their needs have changed a great deal. Shelters still remain places to get out of the rain and the cold or the heat, places that protect those inside from the dangers outside — whatever they maybe. But how those places should look, and how they come to look that way, constantly changes.

The very earliest people did not know how to build buildings. They sheltered themselves in caves. The caves were their homes, their temples and their factories. Yet even a cave could be made beautiful. Some ancient peoples drew lovely pictures on the walls and ceilings of the places where they lived or where they worshipped their gods.

Early people were hunters of animals and gatherers of plant foods. They often had to move to find the animals and the plants they needed. Sometimes they could not find a cave. So they began to make shelters to carry with them: tents made of animal skins, held up by wooden poles.

There are still people who live in tents today. For one reason or another they need to move from place to place. Some of their tents are as small and simple as the earliest tents ever built. And some are large, with several rooms, and beautifully decorated.

As far back as eleven thousand years ago, some people found that if they planted crops and did not have too many animals, they could keep themselves and their animals fed without moving around. These people built lasting shelters. The first ones

were made of whatever was at hand: stones, wood or mud, sometimes made into bricks, with roofs of straw or grass. As a protection from wild animals and from other people, a house, or a whole village of houses, might have a fence in a circle around.

In time, there came to be many such villages, and these villages were drawn together into nations. Villages that were part of a nation tended to have houses that were much alike, partly because the people copied from each other and partly because they had the same building materials to use. Today we call the art of deciding how a building will be built — and how it will look both inside and out — architecture.

The ancient Egyptians began to develop a real style of architecture about six thousand years ago. Trees were very scarce in their country, so they used sun-dried bricks — made from clay — as well as sandstone, limestone and granite as building materials.

Aside from their temples, the most important buildings the Egyptians built were not for living people. They were tombs for the dead. The Egyptians believed in life after death. It was important to them to have a fine residence and all of the things they had enjoyed in life with them after they died. So wealthy nobles built huge, solid tombs, buildings they hoped would last forever. Inside, were their bodies, when they died, and all of the household articles they would want in the next life. Sometimes these were the real things, and sometimes they were just models or paintings on the walls.

The homes of the living Egyptians were not built to last forever. And none of them did. We know what they were like because pictures of them painted on tombs and on temples did last, just as they had hoped.

The first houses the Egyptians made were of palm sticks, put together like a fence, or a sort of screen. Egypt is a warm country. People needed shade and privacy, but not warmth.

After a time, people began to live together in community huts. These had heavy walls made of palms and papyrus, covered with mud. They were mostly places for

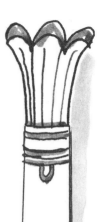

sleeping and eating, because people spent a lot of time out of doors.

But eventually rich and noble people wanted better shelters. So they built houses for just their own families. Made of sandstone and clay bricks, these houses were sometimes two stories high, and had ornamental pillars and flat roofs, and were often decorated with wall carvings and paintings. There were rooms for storing food as well as for cooking, eating, sleeping, bathing and various other activities. Such houses were generally surrounded by walls for privacy and safety.

About three thousand years ago, across the Mediterranean Sea from Egypt, the Greeks began to build their own kinds of buildings. Like the Egyptians, they were not much interested in houses for people, but they did not build huge tombs for the dead either. Instead, they built marble temples for their gods, and theaters and other places where people could meet and talk. Some of these buildings are still thought to be among the most beautiful ever built. Everything was right about them: height, width, length, graceful columns, handsome sloping roofs, and decorations carved or painted onto the walls, showing scenes of Greek life and activities of the gods. Every part of the building blended perfectly with every other part. The Greeks wanted what they built to be as beautiful as possible.

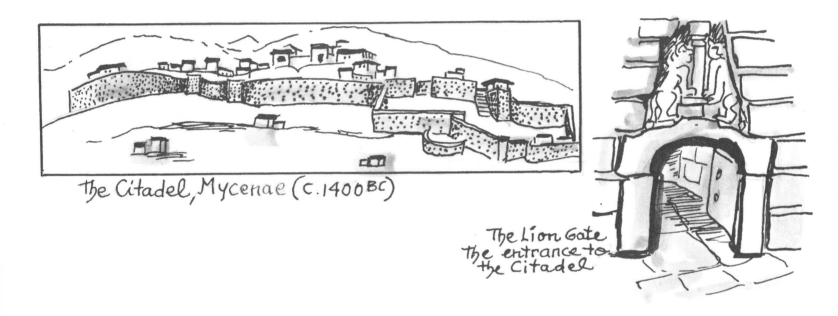

The Citadel, Mycenae (c. 1400 BC)

The Lion Gate the entrance to the Citadel

To the Greek people of those days, life outside the home was more important than life in the home. But this did not mean that their houses could not be comfortable. Many of them were quite large and had many rooms surrounding an open courtyard. They were built of sundried bricks, stone and timber and might be decorated with terracotta (glazed clay). The Greeks also built groups of buildings, homes and stores linked together by sheltered walkways.

By about two thousand years ago, the land around the Mediterranean Sea, including Greece and Egypt, was all controlled by people from the city of Rome, in what is now Italy. The Roman Empire covered much of Europe, the near East and North Africa. When it came to building buildings, the Romans borrowed ideas from all the people they conquered, but especially from the Greeks. The Romans added two main things of their own: arches and domes.

The Romans may have loved beauty, but they loved the power of their empire even more. All of their public buildings everywhere had to be big and strong-looking. Their temples, gymnasiums, public baths, forums where business and government took place, and even their finer homes and villas were made of sturdy bricks, stone and very good cement. The roofs were made of tiles; the walls often were covered with paintings in plaster, called frescoes; and the floors were set in patterns made of stones and small pieces of glass, called mosaics. These buildings were so well built that many of them are still standing.

The Romans planned and built whole towns. They laid out sturdy roads, many of them still in use today. And they brought water to their towns and cities from long distances through huge aqueducts.

But while some Romans lived in large villas with many rooms clustered around a central courtyard, others lived in hovels or in overcrowded apartment buildings. The Romans were the first to build multi-storied apartment houses, but these were not so well constructed. Sometimes they fell down.

Yet, for the most part, just as Greek buildings were beautiful, Roman buildings were sturdy and powerful.

About sixteen hundred years ago the great Roman Empire fell apart. Local areas were left to rule and defend themselves. Times were hard, and the learnings and skills of Greece and Rome were forgotten as people struggled just to survive. At the same time, the people of Europe began to accept the Christian religion. The most important place in each village and town was soon the catherdral, church or monastery. Because Rome was no longer building Roman buildings everywhere, churches in different places looked different. Yet most had Roman arches and Roman rounded ceilings. And some had mosaic or fresco decorations.

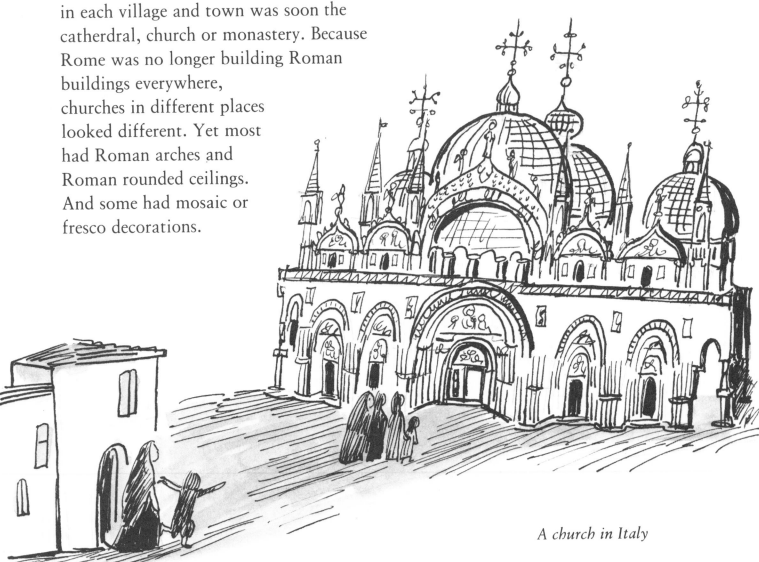

A church in Italy

A church in England

The time after the end of the Roman Empire is often called the Middle Ages. Most people were poor. So, although they built their churches of stone, their houses were made of whatever was easy to find: wood or mud or a combination of the two. Most houses had one large room, where all the activities of living took place.

Peasant cottages were built with flat roofs in places with little rain. In places where rain or snow were part of daily living, the roof was A-shaped, and sometimes made of straw, called a thatched roof. The houses shown are like those built in England at the time.

In some places, houses were built on bridges. A bridge was built over a river, and then small, crowded houses were built on it. This was especially good for merchants, because people who wanted to cross the bridge had to go by the houses and shops. The Ponte Vecchio, still standing in Florence, Italy, was one such bridge.

Castle in Germany

During the Middle Ages, roving bands of robbers and outlaws could appear at any time. So powerful people — kings, lords, knights, and so on — built castles for protection. The family who owned the castle lived in it. The people who lived in the villages around and farmed the land could come to the castle when danger threatened. Castles were built in places that were hard to attack: on a mountaintop or in a lake. They had thick walls, watchtowers (places where defenders of the castle could stand and be protected while they shot their arrows) and riverlike moats with drawbridges over them that could be pulled up to keep people out. How a castle looked depended on where it was built and what dangers it might have to face.

Castle in Switzerland

Castle in Holland

Castle in England

Castle in France

There were castles all over Europe by the end of the Middle Ages. They were probably drafty and uncomfortable to live in. And though they were built for safety and not comfort, they were not always safe. Sometimes they were captured.

Very few castles built in the Middle Ages can be seen today. (Though castles built later can be seen.) Most of them that are still around are in ruins. They did not survive the coming of gunpowder.

A ruin of a castle in France

Although the people of some medieval towns were protected by the local lord and his castle, other townspeople built their own protection. They surrounded their towns with walls that were like castle walls. These had towers, strong gates, and if the way into town was over a bridge, even that was protected. Inside the walls, timber-framed houses huddled close together, like sheep in a sheepfold. Many houses for many people. Buildings of the Middle Ages all seemed to enclose people into small protected areas.

Towns of the Middle Ages had churches. The earliest ones built in the familiar Romanesque style — with heavy walls and round arches. Then about nine hundred years ago, all of this changed. Churches began to reach up. Arches became pointed. Arched ceilings rose to great high points. And tall towers pushed toward the sky, where people of time were sure God lived. The large windows of the new churches were filled with beautiful stained glass that told stories from the Bible and the lives of saints. This new style was called gothic. It started in France, but it soon spread all over Europe, except Italy.

Even houses began to look gothic. It was as if everything built was lifting eyes and thoughts to heaven.

A gothic church and town

While Europe north of Italy was busy building its gothic churches and its castles and walled cities, something else was happening in Italy. People there were rediscovering the art, literature, science and architecture of Greece and Rome. To these old learnings, they were adding their own new learnings. What we now call the Renaissance, which means rebirth, had begun.

Renaissance buildings looked a little like the Greek and Roman buildings of the past. They were not made to defend people, but to look beautiful. They had pillars and, eventually, domes and decorations that made them seem open to the world, not closed in. Yet, though they owed much to the past, they were new — serving a new people in a new time.

The Renaissance was a time of exploring the knowledge of the past, finding new learnings for the present and making discoveries for the future. Sailors went to the Near East, to the Far East, and finally to the West — to the lands that came to be called America.

European settlers went to live in the eastern woodlands of America and found that the people who already lived there made houses of wood, covered with shingles or bark. So the Europeans did the same. But they also used ideas they brought from Europe: fireplaces and windows with leaded glass.

As explorers pushed west in America, they found many kinds of shelters built by Native Americans. Each group of people had created houses that fit their lives and that used what they had available for buildings. Some lived in lodges made of earth or logs. Others had animal skin tents called teepees. Still others lived in round bark houses. And in the Southwest, there were clusters of cubicles — apartment buildings — made of sun-baked earth mixed with water. Many of these houses were beautifully decorated with designs that reminded people of their gods and their ancestors.

The European newcomers borrowed and adapted the architecture of Native Americans. At least the wisest ones did, because the local houses made use of local materials and were adapted to the climate of the place. Yet each group of Europeans used the local ideas in different ways to suit their own needs and ideas.

As some people were exploring and settling the new lands in America, the new ideas in architecture that had developed in Italy were spreading to the north and west in Europe. To show how modern and powerful they were, the kings of France built a great

palace in the Renaissance style. And all over Europe, even amidst wars and hard times, architects created new government buildings, churches and monuments, trying as the Greeks once had, to outdo each other in beauty.

Houses did not change so much. In size and shape they were much like earlier houses, but they took on Renaissance decoration. And in the cities, especially, brick and stone began to replace wood. This was a welcome change because there was less danger of fire. When houses were close together, fires could easily spread from one to the next. So new houses not only looked different but were safer.

New-style houses were built near old-style houses. Towns and cities came to be filled with a mixture of architectures.

As the styles of houses built in Europe gradually began to change, so did the styles of houses built in America. People there were feeling more settled, more secure. And they began to build larger and fancier houses. Many times these were like houses built in the lands from which the builders had come. They used local products, adapted to the forms of Europe.

The Spanish people who settled in the southeastern part of what became the United States, as well as in Central and South America, built Spanish-type houses. The French people in Canada and Louisiana made houses that seemed French, though they were not the elaborate Renaissance buildings of Paris. The English in eastern North America built English-style houses. And the Dutch in New York built Dutch houses.

*Angel at an
Austrian church altar*

People in Europe were feeling wealthy and expansive. So now the Renaissance buildings, too, began to change. Again, the change began in Italy, then spread to France, Austria and other countries. The new style, called baroque, was more elaborate, more full of curves and decorations than anything done before. It seemed to express joy in living. The most important baroque buildings were made in France between 1630 and 1640, but everywhere buildings, and especially churches, began to have the great onion-shaped domes and the joyful decorations that meant baroque.

For a brief time at the end of the baroque period, buildings were given so much ornamentation they were called by a new name, rococo.

Austria:
baroque entrance door

Italy

France

Germany

Spain

England

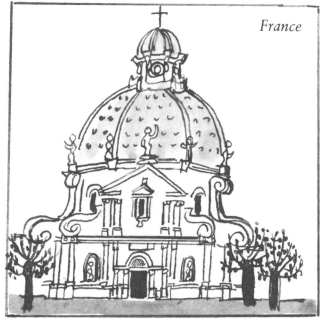

France

As you can see, each country developed its own variety of architecture, to fit its climate and the spirit of its people.

*Russia, too,
had its own style
of baroque.*

When new buildings were erected, old buildings were not torn down, not if they could still be used. So baroque buildings often stood next to Renaissance buildings and to gothic buildings. Sometimes all three styles could be seen, in houses or in public buildings, like a history of architecture, in one very small area.

Times changed. Cities grew larger. And in those cities, factories and business needed to have buildings that were different from anything that had been built before. So gradually, after 1800, new kinds of buildings were designed. Steel beams replaced wood. Cast iron and glass became parts of buildings in new ways.

In Italy, and then in other countries, glass was used to cover wide areas. Glass arches covered large shopping arcades.

Engineers delighted in trying out new shapes, new ways of putting structures together. One result of this was the Eiffel Tower in Paris.

In Liverpool, England, in 1865, an office building was built with an outside of prefabricated cast iron. It was called The Oriol Chambers. Soon such buildings were being built everywhere.

The one invention that changed how buildings looked the most was the elevator. Once Mr. Otis had figured out how to take people from one floor to another by something besides stairs, tall buildings became possible. And elevators along with sturdy steel-beam construction brought in the skyscraper. An early tall building was the Reliance Building in Chicago, constructed in 1894.

As cities grew more and more crowded and land became more and more valuable, buildings both for living and for working grew higher and higher, especially in America. The outside walls no longer held the building up; the steel frame did that, or later the concrete and steel frame. So the outside could simply be hung with thin sheets of aluminum, stone, glass, brick, whatever the builder wanted. Sizes and shapes of such buildings were often determined more by space available, the use to which the place was to be put and the expense of building, than beauty.

As buildings have changed, so have the ways cities are built. Newer cities, those in America especially, have straight avenues going north and south, east and west. Older cities still have avenues and streets leading in many directions from squares and parks. They are more interesting, but also more confusing to strangers.

As always, the houses people live in have changed along with other shelters. New houses have less decoration. They are often simpler both inside and out than older houses. But some of the old remain. And some new houses are made to look like old houses. So our neighborhoods can be made up of many kinds of houses, some for one family and some for many families.

*Art exhibition hall
in Vienna, Austria*

As architects and engineers
experimented with new
ways of building, new styles
of architecture developed.
Victorian houses were very
ornate. Art nouveau
introduced curved lines and
graceful shapes.

*An apartment house
in Barcelona, Spain*

*Office building
in Germany*

Art museum in New York

Habitat in Canada

Post office tower, London

Other new styles have included: the sensitive expressionistic; Bauhaus — very severe and modern — the boxes we see in all our great cities; art deco — the Empire State Building in New York City is in art deco style, adorned with stylized designs. Some new buildings, like Habitat, made for a world's fair in Montreal, are put together in parts. Rooms, or whole apartments, are assembled in one place, and then moved to the place where the building is being built and fastened in.

Restaurant in Los Angeles

Opera house in Sidney, Australia

An apartment house

A Victorian house

A Spanish house

An underground house

A solar house

An A-frame house

Some of the ways we live now.

Row houses

An igloo

Suburban houses

A house on a barge

Modern house

A converted barn

But no matter how different the shelter of today may be from those of yesterday, the people who plan for tomorrow are constantly thinking of still new ways of housing people and their enterprises. There are suggestions for floating houses, floating cities, cities that bridge large canyons, underground cities, and even cities that can be moved from place to place.

And no matter how lovely the shelters and cities of the future may be, good buildings of the past will always look beautiful to us, too. By looking at the fine buildings of the past, we can understand something of what our ancestors were like. And people of tomorrow will look at what we have built and know something about us, about our hopes, our dreams, our lives. For what we build says something about what we are.